GRATITUDE

Scan me

Scan the QR code for free
Instagram story templates
for your daily gratitude practice.

From my heart to your heart - I hope this book
brings you value and makes your reality brighter.
If you enjoyed it, I would be so immensely grateful
if you left a review - let me know how you liked it!
Enjoy your practice & have fun!

Yu Seong
PRESS

Copyright © 2022 Yuseong Press
All rights reserved.

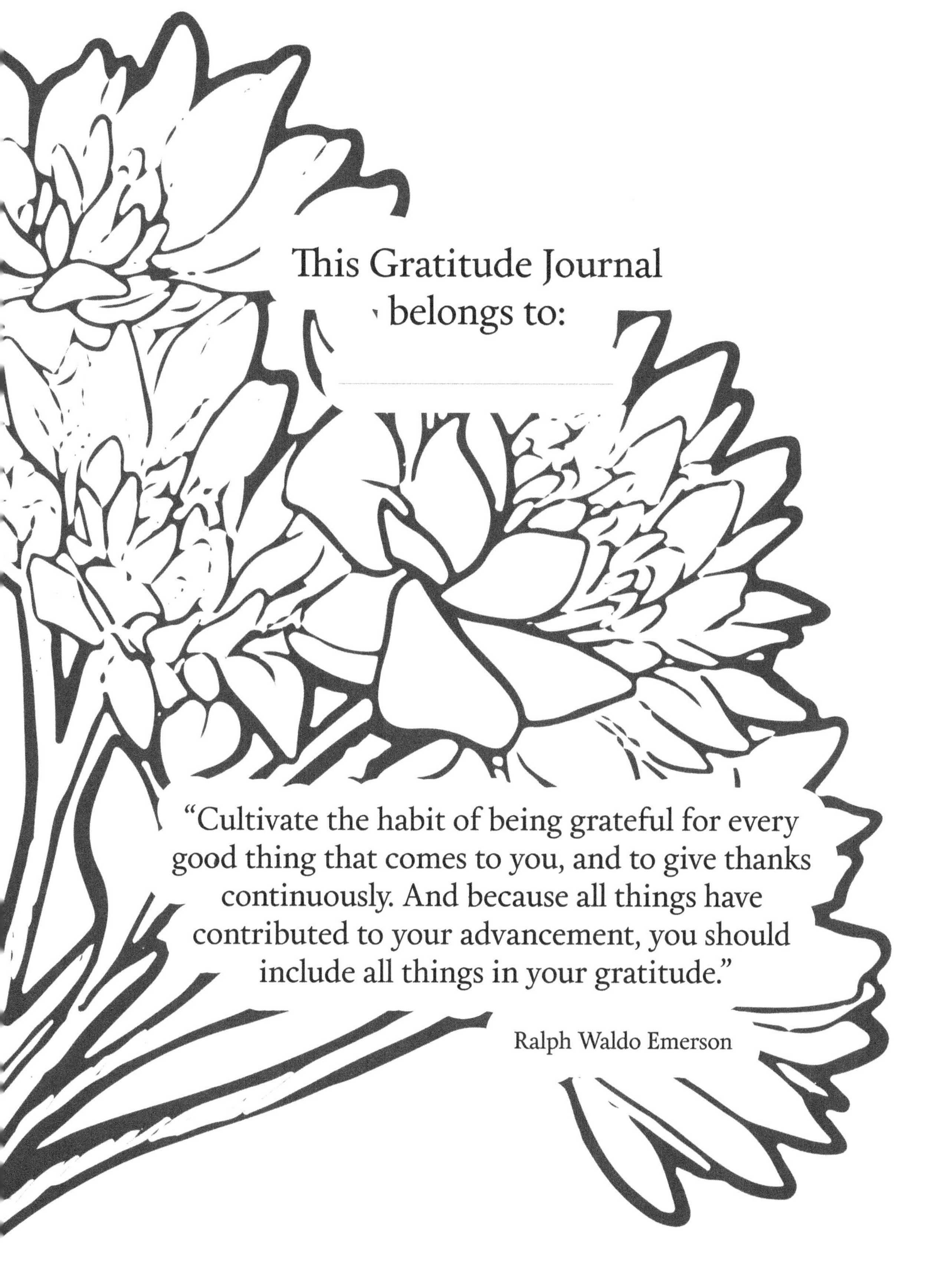
This Gratitude Journal
belongs to:

"Cultivate the habit of being grateful for every
good thing that comes to you, and to give thanks
continuously. And because all things have
contributed to your advancement, you should
include all things in your gratitude."

Ralph Waldo Emerson

Welcome, beautiful! Today begins your new, wonderful journey!

GRATITUDE is a simple, yet powerful feeling that can be practised for free anywhere and anytime. The only thing you need is a pen, paper and a couple of minutes of free time for yourself. No matter how busy your day is, you can find a little window of time and hopefully, this journal will serve as a reminder to reconnect with yourself daily and anchor you in the present moment.

ANY SELF-CARE PRACTICE is a wonderful investment into yourself, and by extension, into your family and all those you care about. Gratitude is an especially powerful tool. Even on the toughest of days, you can think of something to be grateful for and it may be as simple as "I'm breathing", "I had food to eat", "I took a shower". Saying a humble "Thank you" affirms the goodness you are already experiencing and invites more wonderful feelings and situations into your life. In this way, gratitude has the power to transform our lives.

ALL YOU NEED TO DO is to take a deep breath and say "Thank you". Say it a couple of times, for things big and mundane, because all of them are enriching your present life. Spend a couple of moments in this feeling of gratitude.

The time you spend logging your thoughts in this journal is a time you are befriending your own self more deeply. I invite you to become your best friend, your best mate and give yourself this undivided attention. What are you grateful for today? What are you proud of? Delve deeper. Notice how far you have come – be grateful for the opportunities and challenges in your way and see how you have grown and become stronger along the way. The more you reconnect with your inner self and build a strong relationship with yourself, the more clarity and motivation you will gain. Commit to your practice with consistency and dedication, and you will be able to gradually transform your mindset, creating an opening for more good things, and a renewed spark to face any challenges.

According to neuroscience studies, the benefits of gratitude accumulate over time. In one of the studies, participants were asked to write gratitude letters for 90 days and their brain activity was compared with a study group that wasn't practising gratitude. The grateful participants scored noticeably more activity in the medial prefrontal cortex, a brain area associated with learning and decision making. And even without scientific evidence, you can surely notice this correlation yourself: the more you focus your thoughts and feelings on being grateful, the harder it is to stay in a bad mood. It is not easy to hold onto anger or resentment when our attention is devoted to noticing all the blessings in our lives. I encourage you to carry on this experiment in your own life. Be grateful and experience the change by yourself.

All good things take time and great things take a great time. You can start today or tomorrow morning and experience the benefits of a consistent gratitude practice. After 90 days, you can look back into the entries you have logged and see the journey you have taken. Isn't it satisfying to see that you have made the decision to commit to your well-being and no matter what, kept practising? You don't need a magic spell to change your life – the magic is already within you, and it is the power of your decision and action. All great journeys begin with the first step. Invest in yourself, give yourself this great gift.

Are you ready to start your great adventure?

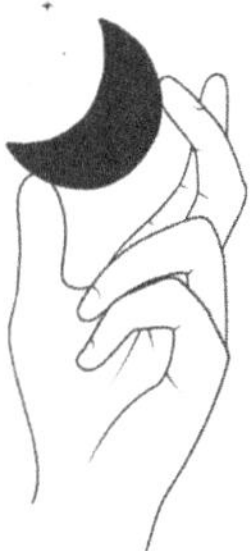

I believe in you!

How to use this gratitude journal?

Each day is divided into a morning and evening section.

Start your day with an affirmation and intention for today and note briefly what you are grateful for.

In the evening, there is more space for you to log your thoughts and reflect on your day and when inspiration strikes you, there is also additional space for journaling and reflections, or even drawing something – let your imagination be unbound!

The journal encourages you to choose a daily affirmation, a power thought to energise you, lift you up and remind you of your strength. On the next page, you will find a couple of affirmations to help you get started and I invite you to come up with your own favorite affirmations that speak to you personally & write them down in the space provided on the following pages. Come back to them as often as you feel you need to.

In between your daily logs, you will find questions-invitations designed to go deeper. As we look into ourselves and back into our life's experience, we notice patterns, propensities, pervasive truths, weak spots. A lot of wisdom is to be gained from self-introspection. Answer as honestly and thoroughly as possible. You can even revisit those questions many times to add more details, as your practice deepens.

At the very end, you will find review questions to be with. Take a couple of moments and see what journey have you taken those weeks. What has changed? Transformation begins with noticing new patterns. Don't forget to be proud of yourself for committing to a self-care practice. Good job!

Last but not least – when in need to relax or be creative, feel free to color the many florals included on the pages of this book.

It is more than okay to skip a day, the important thing is that you keep on returning here – and you are doing this for yourself. You are awesome!

My Affirmations

EVERYTHING ALWAYS WORKS OUT IN MY FAVOR.

I HAVE ALL I NEED TO MAKE TODAY A GREAT DAY.

I KNOW THAT I AM CAPABLE OF LEARNING NEW THINGS.

I AM SAFE AND SUPPORTED.

I CAN RISE ABOVE NEGATIVITY AND STAY CALM IN EVERY MOMENT.

I MAKE GOOD DECISIONS.

I AM PROUD OF MYSELF AND MY ACHIEVEMENTS.

I KNOW THAT I CAN FACE ANY CHALLENGE AND TURN IT INTO
AN OPPORTUNITY.

THERE IS GREAT WEALTH AND ABUNDANCE IN THE WORLD.

I AM WEALTHY.

GOOD FORTUNE FLOWS TO ME.

THE WORLD IS FULL OF KIND AND SUPPORTIVE PEOPLE.

I ACCEPT MY BEAUTY.

MIRACLES HAPPEN IN MY LIFE.

I CHOOSE TO NOTICE BEAUTY AND KINDNESS EVERYWHERE I GO.

I CHOOSE TO BE FULLY PRESENT IN THE NOW.

I EXTEND COMPASSION TOWARDS ALL BEINGS.

I CHOOSE TO CONTRIBUTE MY GIFTS TO THE WORLD.

I AM RICH WITH IDEAS AND INSPIRATION.

I ACCEPT MY GRACE.

I DO THE BEST I CAN EVERY DAY AND I PRAISE MYSELF FOR
MY PERSEVERANCE.

I AM GRATEFUL FOR ALL THAT I HAVE.

My Affirmations

My Affirmations

Mood tracker

DATE: _______________________

Mood Tracker 😀 ☺ 😐 ☹ 😦

Morning

DAILY AFFIRMATION:

I AM GRATEFUL FOR:

MY INTENTION FOR TODAY:

Evening

I AM GRATEFUL FOR:

THREE GOOD THINGS THAT HAPPENED TODAY:

PEOPLE I AM GRATEFUL FOR:

Notes & Reflections

DATE: ______________________

Mood Tracker ☺ ☺ ☺ ☹ ☹

Morning

DAILY AFFIRMATION:

I AM GRATEFUL FOR:

MY INTENTION FOR TODAY:

Evening

I AM GRATEFUL FOR:

THREE GOOD THINGS THAT HAPPENED TODAY:

PEOPLE I AM GRATEFUL FOR:

Notes & Reflections

Mood Tracker 😀 ☺ 😐 ☹ 😣

DATE: ___________________________

Morning

DAILY AFFIRMATION: ___________________________

____

I AM GRATEFUL FOR: ___________________________

____

____

MY INTENTION FOR TODAY: _____________________

____

____

Evening

I AM GRATEFUL FOR: ___________________________

____

____

____

THREE GOOD THINGS THAT HAPPENED TODAY: _____

____

____

____

PEOPLE I AM GRATEFUL FOR: ___________________

____

____

____

What qualities do I love about myself? Why?

DATE: ____________________   Mood Tracker 😃 ☺ 😐 ☹ 😞

Morning

DAILY AFFIRMATION:

I AM GRATEFUL FOR:

MY INTENTION FOR TODAY:

Evening

I AM GRATEFUL FOR:

THREE GOOD THINGS THAT HAPPENED TODAY:

PEOPLE I AM GRATEFUL FOR:

Notes & Reflections

DATE: _______________________

Mood tracker ☺ ☺ ☺ ☹ ☹

Morning

DAILY AFFIRMATION:

____

I AM GRATEFUL FOR:

____

MY INTENTION FOR TODAY:

____

Evening

I AM GRATEFUL FOR:

____

THREE GOOD THINGS THAT HAPPENED TODAY:

____

PEOPLE I AM GRATEFUL FOR:

____

Notes & Reflections

DATE: ____________________   Mood Tracker ☺ ☺ ☺ ☹ ☹

Morning

DAILY AFFIRMATION: ____________________

____

I AM GRATEFUL FOR: ____________________

____

MY INTENTION FOR TODAY: ____________________

____

Evening

I AM GRATEFUL FOR: ____________________

____

____

THREE GOOD THINGS THAT HAPPENED TODAY: ____________________

____

____

PEOPLE I AM GRATEFUL FOR: ____________________

____

____

Notes & Reflections

Mood tracker ☺ ☺ ☐ ☹ ☹

Morning

DAILY AFFIRMATION:

I AM GRATEFUL FOR:

MY INTENTION FOR TODAY:

Evening

I AM GRATEFUL FOR:

THREE GOOD THINGS THAT HAPPENED TODAY:

PEOPLE I AM GRATEFUL FOR:

Notes & Reflections

DATE: ______________________________   *Mood Tracker* 😃 🙂 😐 🙁 😣

Morning

DAILY AFFIRMATION:

I AM GRATEFUL FOR:

MY INTENTION FOR TODAY:

Evening

I AM GRATEFUL FOR:

THREE GOOD THINGS THAT HAPPENED TODAY:

PEOPLE I AM GRATEFUL FOR:

What is my favorite self-care routine that helps me in times of stress?

DATE:

Mood tracker 😀 🙂 😐 🙁 ☹️

Morning

DAILY AFFIRMATION:

I AM GRATEFUL FOR:

MY INTENTION FOR TODAY:

Evening

I AM GRATEFUL FOR:

THREE GOOD THINGS THAT HAPPENED TODAY:

PEOPLE I AM GRATEFUL FOR:

Notes & Reflections

Mood Tracker

DATE:

Morning

DAILY AFFIRMATION:

I AM GRATEFUL FOR:

MY INTENTION FOR TODAY:

Evening

I AM GRATEFUL FOR:

THREE GOOD THINGS THAT HAPPENED TODAY:

PEOPLE I AM GRATEFUL FOR:

What family members am I most grateful for?
What makes them special?

Mood Tracker ☺ ☺ ☺ ☹ ☹

DATE:

Morning

DAILY AFFIRMATION:

I AM GRATEFUL FOR:

MY INTENTION FOR TODAY:

Evening

I AM GRATEFUL FOR:

THREE GOOD THINGS THAT HAPPENED TODAY:

PEOPLE I AM GRATEFUL FOR:

Notes & Reflections

DATE: ___________________ Mood tracker ☺ ☺ ☺ ☹ ☹

Morning

DAILY AFFIRMATION:

I AM GRATEFUL FOR:

MY INTENTION FOR TODAY:

Evening

I AM GRATEFUL FOR:

THREE GOOD THINGS THAT HAPPENED TODAY:

PEOPLE I AM GRATEFUL FOR:

Notes & Reflections

DATE: _______________________   ## Mood Tracker 😀 🙂 😐 🙁 😫

Morning

DAILY AFFIRMATION:

I AM GRATEFUL FOR:

MY INTENTION FOR TODAY:

Evening

I AM GRATEFUL FOR:

THREE GOOD THINGS THAT HAPPENED TODAY:

PEOPLE I AM GRATEFUL FOR:

Notes & Reflections

DATE: _______________________   Mood Tracker 😃 🙂 😐 🙁 😣

Morning

DAILY AFFIRMATION: _______________________

____

I AM GRATEFUL FOR: _______________________

____

MY INTENTION FOR TODAY: _______________________

____

Evening

I AM GRATEFUL FOR: _______________________

____

____

THREE GOOD THINGS THAT HAPPENED TODAY: _______________________

____

____

PEOPLE I AM GRATEFUL FOR: _______________________

____

____

Notes & Reflections

DATE:

Mood Tracker ☺ ☺ ☺ ☹ ☹

Morning

DAILY AFFIRMATION:

I AM GRATEFUL FOR:

MY INTENTION FOR TODAY:

Evening

I AM GRATEFUL FOR:

THREE GOOD THINGS THAT HAPPENED TODAY:

PEOPLE I AM GRATEFUL FOR:

Who special someone has taught me about unconditional love
in the past or present?

DATE: _______________________

Mood Tracker ☺ ☺ 😐 ☹ ☹

Morning

DAILY AFFIRMATION: _______________________

____

____

I AM GRATEFUL FOR: _______________________

____

____

____

MY INTENTION FOR TODAY: ___________________

____

____

Evening

I AM GRATEFUL FOR: _______________________

____

____

____

____

THREE GOOD THINGS THAT HAPPENED TODAY: _____

____

____

____

____

PEOPLE I AM GRATEFUL FOR: _________________

____

____

____

____

Notes & Reflections

DATE: _______________

Mood Tracker ☺ ☺ ☺ ☹ ☹

Morning

DAILY AFFIRMATION:

I AM GRATEFUL FOR:

MY INTENTION FOR TODAY:

Evening

I AM GRATEFUL FOR:

THREE GOOD THINGS THAT HAPPENED TODAY:

PEOPLE I AM GRATEFUL FOR:

Who or what in my life am I happy to let go of?
I will write what I have learned from them and release with gratitude.

Mood Tracker 😃 😊 😐 😟 😣

Morning

DAILY AFFIRMATION:

I AM GRATEFUL FOR:

MY INTENTION FOR TODAY:

Evening

I AM GRATEFUL FOR:

THREE GOOD THINGS THAT HAPPENED TODAY:

PEOPLE I AM GRATEFUL FOR:

Notes & Reflections

DATE:

Morning

DAILY AFFIRMATION:

I AM GRATEFUL FOR:

MY INTENTION FOR TODAY:

Evening

I AM GRATEFUL FOR:

THREE GOOD THINGS THAT HAPPENED TODAY:

PEOPLE I AM GRATEFUL FOR:

Notes & Reflections

DATE: ....

Mood tracker ☺ ☺ ☺ ☹ ☹

Morning

DAILY AFFIRMATION: ....

....

I AM GRATEFUL FOR: ....

....

MY INTENTION FOR TODAY: ....

....

Evening

I AM GRATEFUL FOR: ....

....

....

THREE GOOD THINGS THAT HAPPENED TODAY: ....

....

....

PEOPLE I AM GRATEFUL FOR: ....

....

....

Notes & Reflections

DATE: _______________________

Mood Tracker ☺ ☺ ☺ ☹ ☹

Morning

DAILY AFFIRMATION:

I AM GRATEFUL FOR:

MY INTENTION FOR TODAY:

Evening

I AM GRATEFUL FOR:

THREE GOOD THINGS THAT HAPPENED TODAY:

PEOPLE I AM GRATEFUL FOR:

What do I appreciate about my life?

DATE: ....

Mood tracker 😀 🙂 😐 🙁 ☹️

Morning

DAILY AFFIRMATION: ....

....

I AM GRATEFUL FOR: ....

....

MY INTENTION FOR TODAY: ....

....

Evening

I AM GRATEFUL FOR: ....

....

....

THREE GOOD THINGS THAT HAPPENED TODAY: ....

....

....

PEOPLE I AM GRATEFUL FOR: ....

....

....

Notes & Reflections

Mood Tracker 😀 ☺ 😐 ☹ 😫

Morning

DAILY AFFIRMATION:

I AM GRATEFUL FOR:

MY INTENTION FOR TODAY:

Evening

I AM GRATEFUL FOR:

THREE GOOD THINGS THAT HAPPENED TODAY:

PEOPLE I AM GRATEFUL FOR:

What little victory am I proud of in my life?

DATE: _______________________   Mood tracker ☺ ☺ ☺ ☹ ☹

Morning

DAILY AFFIRMATION:

I AM GRATEFUL FOR:

MY INTENTION FOR TODAY:

Evening

I AM GRATEFUL FOR:

THREE GOOD THINGS THAT HAPPENED TODAY:

PEOPLE I AM GRATEFUL FOR:

Notes & Reflections

Mood Tracker ☺ ☺ ☺ ☹ ☹

Morning

DAILY AFFIRMATION:

I AM GRATEFUL FOR:

MY INTENTION FOR TODAY:

Evening

I AM GRATEFUL FOR:

THREE GOOD THINGS THAT HAPPENED TODAY:

PEOPLE I AM GRATEFUL FOR:

Notes & Reflections

DATE: _______________________

Mood tracker ☺ ☺ ☺ ☹ ☹

Morning

DAILY AFFIRMATION:

I AM GRATEFUL FOR:

MY INTENTION FOR TODAY:

Evening

I AM GRATEFUL FOR:

THREE GOOD THINGS THAT HAPPENED TODAY:

PEOPLE I AM GRATEFUL FOR:

If I were to describe my three best days in detail, they would be as following:

Mood tracker ☺ ☺ ☺ ☹ ☹

Morning

DAILY AFFIRMATION:

I AM GRATEFUL FOR:

MY INTENTION FOR TODAY:

Evening

I AM GRATEFUL FOR:

THREE GOOD THINGS THAT HAPPENED TODAY:

PEOPLE I AM GRATEFUL FOR:

Notes & Reflections

DATE:

Morning

DAILY AFFIRMATION:

I AM GRATEFUL FOR:

MY INTENTION FOR TODAY:

Evening

I AM GRATEFUL FOR:

THREE GOOD THINGS THAT HAPPENED TODAY:

PEOPLE I AM GRATEFUL FOR:

Notes & Reflections

DATE: ____________________

Mood Tracker ☺ ☺ ☺ ☹ ☹

Morning

DAILY AFFIRMATION:

I AM GRATEFUL FOR:

MY INTENTION FOR TODAY:

Evening

I AM GRATEFUL FOR:

THREE GOOD THINGS THAT HAPPENED TODAY:

PEOPLE I AM GRATEFUL FOR:

Three things that always put a smile on my face:

DATE: _______________________   Mood Tracker 😀 🙂 😐 🙁 ☹️

Morning

DAILY AFFIRMATION:

I AM GRATEFUL FOR:

MY INTENTION FOR TODAY:

Evening

I AM GRATEFUL FOR:

THREE GOOD THINGS THAT HAPPENED TODAY:

PEOPLE I AM GRATEFUL FOR:

Notes & Reflections

Mood Tracker 😀 🙂 😐 🙁 ☹️

DATE: _______________

Morning

DAILY AFFIRMATION:

I AM GRATEFUL FOR:

MY INTENTION FOR TODAY:

Evening

I AM GRATEFUL FOR:

THREE GOOD THINGS THAT HAPPENED TODAY:

PEOPLE I AM GRATEFUL FOR:

Notes & Reflections

DATE: _______________   # Mood tracker 😃 🙂 😐 🙁 😣

Morning

DAILY AFFIRMATION: _______________________________

____

I AM GRATEFUL FOR: _______________________________

____

MY INTENTION FOR TODAY: __________________________

____

Evening

I AM GRATEFUL FOR: _______________________________

____

____

____

THREE GOOD THINGS THAT HAPPENED TODAY: ___________

____

____

____

PEOPLE I AM GRATEFUL FOR: _________________________

____

____

Who makes me feel loved and why?

DATE: _______________

Morning

DAILY AFFIRMATION:

I AM GRATEFUL FOR:

MY INTENTION FOR TODAY:

Evening

I AM GRATEFUL FOR:

THREE GOOD THINGS THAT HAPPENED TODAY:

PEOPLE I AM GRATEFUL FOR:

Notes & Reflections

DATE: _______________________

Mood Tracker ☺ ☺ ☺ ☹ ☹

Morning

DAILY AFFIRMATION: _______________________

I AM GRATEFUL FOR:

MY INTENTION FOR TODAY:

Evening

I AM GRATEFUL FOR:

THREE GOOD THINGS THAT HAPPENED TODAY:

PEOPLE I AM GRATEFUL FOR:

Notes & Reflections

DATE: _______________   *Mood Tracker* 😀 ☺ 😐 ☹ 😧

Morning

DAILY AFFIRMATION:

I AM GRATEFUL FOR:

MY INTENTION FOR TODAY:

Evening

I AM GRATEFUL FOR:

THREE GOOD THINGS THAT HAPPENED TODAY:

PEOPLE I AM GRATEFUL FOR:

Notes & Reflections

DATE: ....

Mood Tracker 😃 🙂 😐 🙁 😣

Morning

DAILY AFFIRMATION: ....

....

I AM GRATEFUL FOR: ....

....

MY INTENTION FOR TODAY: ....

....

Evening

I AM GRATEFUL FOR: ....

....

THREE GOOD THINGS THAT HAPPENED TODAY: ....

....

PEOPLE I AM GRATEFUL FOR: ....

....

Notes & Reflections

DATE: Mood Tracker ☺ ☺ ☺ ☹ ☹

Morning

DAILY AFFIRMATION:

I AM GRATEFUL FOR:

MY INTENTION FOR TODAY:

Evening

I AM GRATEFUL FOR:

THREE GOOD THINGS THAT HAPPENED TODAY:

PEOPLE I AM GRATEFUL FOR:

What makes me feel calm and relaxed?

DATE: ....

Mood tracker 😃 ☺ 😐 🙁 ☹

Morning

DAILY AFFIRMATION:

I AM GRATEFUL FOR:

MY INTENTION FOR TODAY:

Evening

I AM GRATEFUL FOR:

THREE GOOD THINGS THAT HAPPENED TODAY:

PEOPLE I AM GRATEFUL FOR:

Notes & Reflections

DATE: _______________________   Mood Tracker 😀 🙂 😐 🙁 😫

Morning

DAILY AFFIRMATION:

I AM GRATEFUL FOR:

MY INTENTION FOR TODAY:

Evening

I AM GRATEFUL FOR:

THREE GOOD THINGS THAT HAPPENED TODAY:

PEOPLE I AM GRATEFUL FOR:

Mood tracker 😀 🙂 😐 🙁 😣

Morning

DAILY AFFIRMATION:

I AM GRATEFUL FOR:

MY INTENTION FOR TODAY:

Evening

I AM GRATEFUL FOR:

THREE GOOD THINGS THAT HAPPENED TODAY:

PEOPLE I AM GRATEFUL FOR:

What have I seen recently that warmed my heart?

Mood Tracker ☺ ☺ ☺ ☹ ☹

Morning

DAILY AFFIRMATION:

I AM GRATEFUL FOR:

MY INTENTION FOR TODAY:

Evening

I AM GRATEFUL FOR:

THREE GOOD THINGS THAT HAPPENED TODAY:

PEOPLE I AM GRATEFUL FOR:

Notes & Reflections

Mood Tracker ☺ ☺ ☺ ☹ ☹

Morning

DAILY AFFIRMATION:

I AM GRATEFUL FOR:

MY INTENTION FOR TODAY:

Evening

I AM GRATEFUL FOR:

THREE GOOD THINGS THAT HAPPENED TODAY:

PEOPLE I AM GRATEFUL FOR:

Notes & Reflections

Mood Tracker ☺ ☺ 😐 ☹ ☹

Morning

DAILY AFFIRMATION:

I AM GRATEFUL FOR:

MY INTENTION FOR TODAY:

Evening

I AM GRATEFUL FOR:

THREE GOOD THINGS THAT HAPPENED TODAY:

PEOPLE I AM GRATEFUL FOR:

Notes & Reflections

DATE: _______________________

Mood Tracker ☺ ☺ ☺ ☹ ☹

Morning

DAILY AFFIRMATION:

I AM GRATEFUL FOR:

MY INTENTION FOR TODAY:

Evening

I AM GRATEFUL FOR:

THREE GOOD THINGS THAT HAPPENED TODAY:

PEOPLE I AM GRATEFUL FOR:

What am I grateful for in my current job?

Mood tracker 😀 🙂 😐 ☹️ 😣

Morning

DAILY AFFIRMATION:

I AM GRATEFUL FOR:

MY INTENTION FOR TODAY:

Evening

I AM GRATEFUL FOR:

THREE GOOD THINGS THAT HAPPENED TODAY:

PEOPLE I AM GRATEFUL FOR:

Notes & Reflections

Mood Tracker ☺ ☺ ☺ ☹ ☹

Morning

DAILY AFFIRMATION:

I AM GRATEFUL FOR:

MY INTENTION FOR TODAY:

Evening

I AM GRATEFUL FOR:

THREE GOOD THINGS THAT HAPPENED TODAY:

PEOPLE I AM GRATEFUL FOR:

Notes & Reflections

DATE: ______________________________   Mood Tracker ☺ ☺ ☺ ☹ ☹

Morning

DAILY AFFIRMATION:

I AM GRATEFUL FOR:

MY INTENTION FOR TODAY:

Evening

I AM GRATEFUL FOR:

THREE GOOD THINGS THAT HAPPENED TODAY:

PEOPLE I AM GRATEFUL FOR:

Which season do I enjoy the most and why?

DATE: ________________________   # Mood tracker ☺ ☺ ☺ ☹ ☹

Morning

DAILY AFFIRMATION:

I AM GRATEFUL FOR:

MY INTENTION FOR TODAY:

Evening

I AM GRATEFUL FOR:

THREE GOOD THINGS THAT HAPPENED TODAY:

PEOPLE I AM GRATEFUL FOR:

What do I appreciate about the place I live in right now?

Mood Tracker ☺ ☺ ☺ ☹ ☹

Morning

DAILY AFFIRMATION:

I AM GRATEFUL FOR:

MY INTENTION FOR TODAY:

Evening

I AM GRATEFUL FOR:

THREE GOOD THINGS THAT HAPPENED TODAY:

PEOPLE I AM GRATEFUL FOR:

Notes & Reflections

DATE: _______________________   Mood tracker 😀 🙂 😐 🙁 ☹️

Morning

DAILY AFFIRMATION:

I AM GRATEFUL FOR:

MY INTENTION FOR TODAY:

Evening

I AM GRATEFUL FOR:

THREE GOOD THINGS THAT HAPPENED TODAY:

PEOPLE I AM GRATEFUL FOR:

Ten things that I am grateful for right now:

DATE: _______________

Mood Tracker ☺ ☺ ☺ ☹ ☹

Morning

DAILY AFFIRMATION:

I AM GRATEFUL FOR:

MY INTENTION FOR TODAY:

Evening

I AM GRATEFUL FOR:

THREE GOOD THINGS THAT HAPPENED TODAY:

PEOPLE I AM GRATEFUL FOR:

DATE:

Mood tracker ☺ ☺ ☺ ☹ ☹

Morning

DAILY AFFIRMATION:

I AM GRATEFUL FOR:

MY INTENTION FOR TODAY:

Evening

I AM GRATEFUL FOR:

THREE GOOD THINGS THAT HAPPENED TODAY:

PEOPLE I AM GRATEFUL FOR:

Notes & Reflections

DATE: _______________________

Mood Tracker ☺ ☺ ☺ ☹ ☹

Morning

DAILY AFFIRMATION:

I AM GRATEFUL FOR:

MY INTENTION FOR TODAY:

Evening

I AM GRATEFUL FOR:

THREE GOOD THINGS THAT HAPPENED TODAY:

PEOPLE I AM GRATEFUL FOR:

Five positive changes I have made in my life:

DATE: _______________________   Mood tracker ☺ ☺ ☺ ☹ ☹

Morning

DAILY AFFIRMATION: ____________________________

____

I AM GRATEFUL FOR: ____________________________

____

MY INTENTION FOR TODAY: ______________________

____

Evening

I AM GRATEFUL FOR: ____________________________

____

____

____

THREE GOOD THINGS THAT HAPPENED TODAY: ______

____

____

____

PEOPLE I AM GRATEFUL FOR: _____________________

____

____

____

Notes & Reflections

Mood Tracker 😃 😊 😐 ☹️ 😣

Morning

DAILY AFFIRMATION:

I AM GRATEFUL FOR:

MY INTENTION FOR TODAY:

Evening

I AM GRATEFUL FOR:

THREE GOOD THINGS THAT HAPPENED TODAY:

PEOPLE I AM GRATEFUL FOR:

What makes me laugh every time I hear it?

DATE: _______________________   Mood tracker 😀 ☺ 😐 🙁 😫

Morning

DAILY AFFIRMATION:

I AM GRATEFUL FOR:

MY INTENTION FOR TODAY:

Evening

I AM GRATEFUL FOR:

THREE GOOD THINGS THAT HAPPENED TODAY:

PEOPLE I AM GRATEFUL FOR:

Notes & Reflections

DATE: ______________________

Mood Tracker ☺ ☺ ☺ ☹ ☹

Morning

DAILY AFFIRMATION:

I AM GRATEFUL FOR:

MY INTENTION FOR TODAY:

Evening

I AM GRATEFUL FOR:

THREE GOOD THINGS THAT HAPPENED TODAY:

PEOPLE I AM GRATEFUL FOR:

What do I look forward to doing in my free time?

DATE: _______________________________

Mood Tracker ☺ ☺ ☺ ☹ ☹

Morning

DAILY AFFIRMATION:

I AM GRATEFUL FOR:

MY INTENTION FOR TODAY:

Evening

I AM GRATEFUL FOR:

THREE GOOD THINGS THAT HAPPENED TODAY:

PEOPLE I AM GRATEFUL FOR:

Notes & Reflections

Morning

DAILY AFFIRMATION:

I AM GRATEFUL FOR:

MY INTENTION FOR TODAY:

Evening

I AM GRATEFUL FOR:

THREE GOOD THINGS THAT HAPPENED TODAY:

PEOPLE I AM GRATEFUL FOR:

What about nature am I grateful for?

DATE: ____________________   Mood tracker   😀 🙂 😐 🙁 😫

Morning

DAILY AFFIRMATION:

I AM GRATEFUL FOR:

MY INTENTION FOR TODAY:

Evening

I AM GRATEFUL FOR:

THREE GOOD THINGS THAT HAPPENED TODAY:

PEOPLE I AM GRATEFUL FOR:

Notes & Reflections

DATE: _______________________   ## Mood Tracker ☺ ☺ ☺ ☹ ☹

Morning

DAILY AFFIRMATION:

I AM GRATEFUL FOR:

MY INTENTION FOR TODAY:

Evening

I AM GRATEFUL FOR:

THREE GOOD THINGS THAT HAPPENED TODAY:

PEOPLE I AM GRATEFUL FOR:

When was that time when a faithful friend has listened to my troubles and made me feel better? What makes my friends special?

Mood Tracker ☺ ☺ ☺ ☹ ☹

Morning

DAILY AFFIRMATION:

I AM GRATEFUL FOR:

MY INTENTION FOR TODAY:

Evening

I AM GRATEFUL FOR:

THREE GOOD THINGS THAT HAPPENED TODAY:

PEOPLE I AM GRATEFUL FOR:

Notes & Reflections

DATE: _______________________

Mood Tracker ☺ ☺ 😐 ☹ ☹

Morning

DAILY AFFIRMATION:

I AM GRATEFUL FOR:

MY INTENTION FOR TODAY:

Evening

I AM GRATEFUL FOR:

THREE GOOD THINGS THAT HAPPENED TODAY:

PEOPLE I AM GRATEFUL FOR:

Notes & Reflections

DATE: ______________________

Mood tracker 😀 ☺ 😐 ☹ 😖

Morning

DAILY AFFIRMATION:

____

____

I AM GRATEFUL FOR:

____

____

MY INTENTION FOR TODAY:

____

____

Evening

I AM GRATEFUL FOR:

____

____

____

THREE GOOD THINGS THAT HAPPENED TODAY:

____

____

____

PEOPLE I AM GRATEFUL FOR:

____

____

____

Notes & Reflections

DATE:

Mood Tracker ☺ ☺ ☺ ☹ ☹

Morning

DAILY AFFIRMATION:

I AM GRATEFUL FOR:

MY INTENTION FOR TODAY:

Evening

I AM GRATEFUL FOR:

THREE GOOD THINGS THAT HAPPENED TODAY:

PEOPLE I AM GRATEFUL FOR:

What luxury do I have in my life?

DATE: _______________________   Mood tracker ☺ ☺ ☺ ☹ ☹

Morning

DAILY AFFIRMATION:

I AM GRATEFUL FOR:

MY INTENTION FOR TODAY:

Evening

I AM GRATEFUL FOR:

THREE GOOD THINGS THAT HAPPENED TODAY:

PEOPLE I AM GRATEFUL FOR:

Notes & Reflections

DATE:

Mood tracker ☺ ☺ ☺ ☹ ☹

Morning

DAILY AFFIRMATION:

I AM GRATEFUL FOR:

MY INTENTION FOR TODAY:

Evening

I AM GRATEFUL FOR:

THREE GOOD THINGS THAT HAPPENED TODAY:

PEOPLE I AM GRATEFUL FOR:

Three things about my body that I love:

DATE: ____________________________ Mood Tracker ☺ ☺ ☺ ☹ ☹

Morning

DAILY AFFIRMATION:

I AM GRATEFUL FOR:

MY INTENTION FOR TODAY:

Evening

I AM GRATEFUL FOR:

THREE GOOD THINGS THAT HAPPENED TODAY:

PEOPLE I AM GRATEFUL FOR:

Notes & Reflections

DATE: _______________________   Mood Tracker 😀 ☺ 😐 ☹ 😦

Morning

DAILY AFFIRMATION:

I AM GRATEFUL FOR:

MY INTENTION FOR TODAY:

Evening

I AM GRATEFUL FOR:

THREE GOOD THINGS THAT HAPPENED TODAY:

PEOPLE I AM GRATEFUL FOR:

Notes & Reflections

DATE: ___________________

Mood Tracker 😀 🙂 😐 🙁 ☹️

Morning

DAILY AFFIRMATION:

I AM GRATEFUL FOR:

MY INTENTION FOR TODAY:

Evening

I AM GRATEFUL FOR:

THREE GOOD THINGS THAT HAPPENED TODAY:

PEOPLE I AM GRATEFUL FOR:

What accomplishment am I proud of?

DATE: _______________________   Mood Tracker ☺ ☺ ☺ ☹ ☹

Morning

DAILY AFFIRMATION:

I AM GRATEFUL FOR:

MY INTENTION FOR TODAY:

Evening

I AM GRATEFUL FOR:

THREE GOOD THINGS THAT HAPPENED TODAY:

PEOPLE I AM GRATEFUL FOR:

Notes & Reflections

DATE: ______________________   Mood tracker 😀 ☺ 😐 ☹ 😞

Morning

DAILY AFFIRMATION:

I AM GRATEFUL FOR:

MY INTENTION FOR TODAY:

Evening

I AM GRATEFUL FOR:

THREE GOOD THINGS THAT HAPPENED TODAY:

PEOPLE I AM GRATEFUL FOR:

What is my favorite part of my daily routine?

Mood Tracker ☺ ☺ ☺ ☹ ☹

Morning

DAILY AFFIRMATION:

I AM GRATEFUL FOR:

MY INTENTION FOR TODAY:

Evening

I AM GRATEFUL FOR:

THREE GOOD THINGS THAT HAPPENED TODAY:

PEOPLE I AM GRATEFUL FOR:

Notes & Reflections

DATE: ______________________   Mood tracker 😃 🙂 😐 🙁 😧

Morning

DAILY AFFIRMATION:

I AM GRATEFUL FOR:

MY INTENTION FOR TODAY:

Evening

I AM GRATEFUL FOR:

THREE GOOD THINGS THAT HAPPENED TODAY:

PEOPLE I AM GRATEFUL FOR:

That time when someone went out of their way to help me was:

DATE: Mood Tracker ☺ ☺ ☺ ☹ ☹

Morning

DAILY AFFIRMATION:

I AM GRATEFUL FOR:

MY INTENTION FOR TODAY:

Evening

I AM GRATEFUL FOR:

THREE GOOD THINGS THAT HAPPENED TODAY:

PEOPLE I AM GRATEFUL FOR:

Mood Tracker ☺ ☺ 😐 ☹ ☹

Morning

DAILY AFFIRMATION:

I AM GRATEFUL FOR:

MY INTENTION FOR TODAY:

Evening

I AM GRATEFUL FOR:

THREE GOOD THINGS THAT HAPPENED TODAY:

PEOPLE I AM GRATEFUL FOR:

Notes & Reflections

DATE:

Mood Tracker ☺ ☺ ☺ ☹ ☹

Morning

DAILY AFFIRMATION:

I AM GRATEFUL FOR:

MY INTENTION FOR TODAY:

Evening

I AM GRATEFUL FOR:

THREE GOOD THINGS THAT HAPPENED TODAY:

PEOPLE I AM GRATEFUL FOR:

That time when I went out of my way to help someone was:

Mood Tracker ☺ ☺ ☺ ☹ ☹

Morning

DAILY AFFIRMATION:

I AM GRATEFUL FOR:

MY INTENTION FOR TODAY:

Evening

I AM GRATEFUL FOR:

THREE GOOD THINGS THAT HAPPENED TODAY:

PEOPLE I AM GRATEFUL FOR:

What makes me feel excited?

DATE: _______________

Mood Tracker ☻ ☺ ☺ ☹ ☹

Morning

DAILY AFFIRMATION:

I AM GRATEFUL FOR:

MY INTENTION FOR TODAY:

Evening

I AM GRATEFUL FOR:

THREE GOOD THINGS THAT HAPPENED TODAY:

PEOPLE I AM GRATEFUL FOR:

What is my happiest childhood memory?

DATE: _______________________

Mood Tracker ☺ ☺ 😐 ☹ ☹

Morning

DAILY AFFIRMATION:

I AM GRATEFUL FOR:

MY INTENTION FOR TODAY:

Evening

I AM GRATEFUL FOR:

THREE GOOD THINGS THAT HAPPENED TODAY:

PEOPLE I AM GRATEFUL FOR:

Notes & Reflections

DATE: _______________________

Mood tracker ☺ ☺ 😐 ☹ ☹

Morning

DAILY AFFIRMATION:

I AM GRATEFUL FOR:

MY INTENTION FOR TODAY:

Evening

I AM GRATEFUL FOR:

THREE GOOD THINGS THAT HAPPENED TODAY:

PEOPLE I AM GRATEFUL FOR:

Notes & Reflections

DATE: _______________________

Mood Tracker ☺ ☺ ☺ ☹ ☹

Morning

DAILY AFFIRMATION: _______________________

____

I AM GRATEFUL FOR: _______________________

____

____

MY INTENTION FOR TODAY: _______________________

____

____

Evening

I AM GRATEFUL FOR: _______________________

____

____

____

THREE GOOD THINGS THAT HAPPENED TODAY: _______________

____

____

____

PEOPLE I AM GRATEFUL FOR: _______________________

____

____

Something weird or random that brings me joy:

Mood Tracker ☺ ☺ 😐 ☹ ☹

Morning

DAILY AFFIRMATION:

I AM GRATEFUL FOR:

MY INTENTION FOR TODAY:

Evening

I AM GRATEFUL FOR:

THREE GOOD THINGS THAT HAPPENED TODAY:

PEOPLE I AM GRATEFUL FOR:

Notes & Reflections

DATE:

Mood Tracker ☺ ☺ ☺ ☹ ☹

Morning

DAILY AFFIRMATION:

I AM GRATEFUL FOR:

MY INTENTION FOR TODAY:

Evening

I AM GRATEFUL FOR:

THREE GOOD THINGS THAT HAPPENED TODAY:

PEOPLE I AM GRATEFUL FOR:

What is my most exciting adventure?

DATE:

Mood Tracker 😃 ☺ 😐 ☹ 😞

Morning

DAILY AFFIRMATION:

I AM GRATEFUL FOR:

MY INTENTION FOR TODAY:

Evening

I AM GRATEFUL FOR:

THREE GOOD THINGS THAT HAPPENED TODAY:

PEOPLE I AM GRATEFUL FOR:

The best three things that I have eaten this week:

DATE: _______________________

Mood tracker ☺ ☺ ☺ ☹ ☹

Morning

DAILY AFFIRMATION:

I AM GRATEFUL FOR:

MY INTENTION FOR TODAY:

Evening

I AM GRATEFUL FOR:

THREE GOOD THINGS THAT HAPPENED TODAY:

PEOPLE I AM GRATEFUL FOR:

What is a tradition I love and look forward to every year?
What makes it special to me?

DATE: ___________________________   Mood tracker ☺ ☺ ☺ ☹ ☹

Morning

DAILY AFFIRMATION:

I AM GRATEFUL FOR:

MY INTENTION FOR TODAY:

Evening

I AM GRATEFUL FOR:

THREE GOOD THINGS THAT HAPPENED TODAY:

PEOPLE I AM GRATEFUL FOR:

Notes & Reflections

DATE: ________________________

Mood Tracker ☺ ☺ ☺ ☹ ☹

Morning

DAILY AFFIRMATION: ____________________

____

I AM GRATEFUL FOR: ____________________

____

MY INTENTION FOR TODAY: ________________

____

Evening

I AM GRATEFUL FOR: ____________________

____

THREE GOOD THINGS THAT HAPPENED TODAY: ___

____

PEOPLE I AM GRATEFUL FOR: ______________

____

Where is my favorite place in the world?

DATE: _______________________   # Mood tracker ☺ ☺ ☺ ☹ ☹

Morning

DAILY AFFIRMATION:

____

____

I AM GRATEFUL FOR:

____

____

MY INTENTION FOR TODAY:

____

____

Evening

I AM GRATEFUL FOR:

____

____

____

____

THREE GOOD THINGS THAT HAPPENED TODAY:

____

____

____

PEOPLE I AM GRATEFUL FOR:

____

____

____

____

What does my ideal day look like? What makes me feel happy and fulfilled?

DATE: ____________________   Morning Tracker ☺ ☺ ☺ ☹ ☹

Morning

DAILY AFFIRMATION: ____

____

I AM GRATEFUL FOR: ____

____

MY INTENTION FOR TODAY: ____

____

____

Evening

I AM GRATEFUL FOR: ____

____

____

____

THREE GOOD THINGS THAT HAPPENED TODAY: __________________________

____

____

____

PEOPLE I AM GRATEFUL FOR: _______________________________________

____

____

The last time I truly felt at peace was:

Review

I am proud of myself for:

Review

What have I learned about myself?

Review

What has changed in my life?

Is there anything I feel I need to let go of? Why?

Review

What makes me feel excited?
What goals and dreams do I want to tackle?

www.ingramcontent.com/pod-product-compliance
Lightning Source LLC
Chambersburg PA
CBHW081339160726
48000CB00010B/3156